## DATE DUE

| | | |
|---|---|---|
| APR 22 1997 | | |
| FE 24 '03 | | |
| JA 10 '06 | | |
| AP 17 '07 | | |
| AP 23 07 | | |
| | | |
| | | |
| | | |
| | | |
| | | |
| | | |
| | | |
| | | |
| | | |
| | | |
| | | |
| | | |
| | | |
| | | |
| | | |
| GAYLORD | | PRINTED IN U S A |

# Military Aircraft Library
## Airlift

# Military Aircraft Library
# Airlift

**DR. DAVID BAKER**

**Rourke Enterprises, Inc.**
**Vero Beach, FL 32964**

**Library of Congress Cataloging-in-Publication Data**

Baker, David, 1944-
  Airlift/by David Baker.

    p. cm. — (The Military aircraft series)
    Includes index.
    Summary: Traces the development of cargo planes and
describes their uses in peace and wartime missions.
    ISBN 0-86592-531-3
    1. Transport planes — United States — Juvenile literature
2. Airlift, Military — United States — Juvenile literature.
[1. Transport planes.  2. Airlifts, Military.  3. Airplanes.]
I. Title.   II. Series: Baker, David, 1944-          Military
aircraft Library.
UG1242.T7B35   1989            88-32664
358.4′4 — dc19                           CIP
                                         AC

# CONTENTS

1    **The Big Lift**         6

2    **Freighters**         17

3    **The Giants**         30

4    **Future Freighters**         43

    **Glossary**         46

    **Index**         48

# The Big Lift

Cargo planes are not the most exciting aircraft operated by the U.S. Air Force. They are usually big and sometimes ugly. They spend their lives flying back and forth between military bases with tons of cargo or people. Yet for all that, transport planes are just as important as bombers and fighters. If the transport planes were unable to fly, the men and machines that make up the U.S. Army, Navy, Air Force and Marine Corp would quickly grind to a halt.

Without the regular supply of materials, ammunition, men, and machines, the military services would be useless. In peacetime, equipment can be sent by road, rail, or ship. In wartime, troops cannot wait for ship loads of supplies, and most of the supplies have to go by air. The air force operates about 1,800 planes for transporting these supplies wherever they are needed, anywhere on earth.

Because of its defense agreements and international responsibilities, the United States has about 460,000 servicemen and women in foreign countries. An additional 64,000 are afloat with the navy. Most of these army and air force personnel

*The Lockheed C-5 Galaxy is the largest transport plane presently operated by the air force.*

serve at stations in Europe and the Far East, and their planes, tanks, guns, and stores need regular replenishment.

It has not always been this way. During World War Two (1939-45), the U.S. Air Force relied on converted airliners or civil transport planes to lift men and machines across the country. When U.S. soldiers went to fight in Europe, most cargo went by sea. This was also true for the navy and the marines in the Pacific. Immediately after the war, the United

*Shortly after World War Two, Soviet occupation of Eastern Europe led to tension in Berlin and transport planes were necessary to fly supplies in.*

*One of the most commonly used aircraft during the Berlin Airlift was the C-47, a plane later used in Vietnam.*

*The C-47 was a military version of the Douglas DC-3 airliner developed in the early 1930s.*

States helped Europe with food, medical supplies, and clothing.

The war had left most European countries without money, decent food, or medicines. The factories had been occupied solely with producing weapons, and now these countries had run out of essential materials. At the end of the war, the Russians occupied East Germany as well as several other eastern European countries. They refused to go back to their old boundaries. The Russian occupation of East Germany included the old

German capital city of Berlin. They allowed people from West Germany to use road and rail links into the city.

Suddenly, in June 1948, the Russians refused to allow road, rail, and barge traffic from the West to pass through East Germany on its way to Berlin, which was occupied by the Americans, the British, and the French as well as the Russians. All four had their own sectors of the city, and without supplies the people of Berlin in the American, British and French sectors were completely cut off. They were

totally isolated and would have starved without food and provisions.

The United States and Britain immediately began an airlift, flying in supplies around the clock using any available military transport plane. The U.S. Air Force had two main types of cargo planes. These were the C-47 and the C-54. All U.S. transport aircraft had the prefix "C" for cargo. The C-47 was the transport version of the famous Douglas DC-3

*The C-47 was one of the most successful early air force transport planes.*

*Although still flying, the C-47 is no longer in service with the air force.*

*Developed during World War Two, the C-54 was also operated as a commercial airliner known as the DC-4.*

Dakota. First flown in 1935, the DC-3 was as important as the first flight of a powered aircraft had been in 1903 when the *Wright brothers* took to the air.

The DC-3 transformed aviation because it opened up routine air transport and proved adaptable to a very wide range of duties. Douglas built 10,654 Dakotas between 1935 and 1947, and all but 458 were used for military duties. The twin-engined Dakota was known as the C-47 in the transport role and played a major part in the *Berlin Airlift*, as the relief operation for the old German capital was called. It was capable of lifting 3 tons of cargo or 28 fully equipped troops. Cruising speed was about 160 MPH and range about 1,600 miles.

*Another Douglas aircraft, the C-54, came into service during the 1940s.*

The most widely used plane during the Berlin Airlift was the Douglas C-54 Skymaster, the military cargo version of the DC-4. The Skymaster was bigger than the DC-3, had four engines, and could carry 50 troops or 16 tons of cargo at a speed of 200 MPH. The C-54 had a side-loading door like the C-47, and moving large crates of supplies in and out of the fuselage was a difficult process. Nevertheless, 1,163 were built between 1942 and 1946 and they helped

11

move more than 1.7 million tons of supplies into Berlin between June 1948, and September 1949. The British flew in an extra 542,000 tons.

The Berlin Airlift was an enormous success. It kept Berliners and foreign troops fed, watered, and clothed for more than a year when the Russians blockaded the supply routes. It also showed the U.S. Air Force what it would have to prepare for in the future. Soviet occupation of East Germany, Bulgaria, Czechoslovakia, Hungary, Poland, and Rumania was a possible threat to freedom in western European countries, including Germany, Italy, France, Belgium, Denmark, the Netherlands, and Great Britain.

The U.S. Air Force wanted bigger transport planes with greater carrying capacity. Two planes, designed during World War Two, were coming into service. One was the Douglas C-74 Globemaster I. It was specially built to carry up to 125 troops, 115 stretchers and medical attendants, or 24 tons of cargo. It was a big step beyond the C-54 and came into service during 1947.

Because the war ended before production began, only 14 C-74s were ever built. The C-74 did pioneer one major improvement the cargo handlers

*Operated by the air force immediately after World War Two, the Douglas C-74 Globemaster I failed to see wide operational use.*

*The B-29 Superfortress bomber of World War Two became the basis for the next air force transport plane.*

approved of — an electric lift to raise cargo straight into the undersection of the fuselage and two cranes, each capable of lifting 4-ton loads. The C-74 got itself into the history books when, on November 18, 1949, it became the first plane to carry more than 100 people across the Atlantic.

The second large transport plane designed during the war was a converted Boeing B-29 Superfortress.

As a bomber, the B-29 pounded Japanese soldiers on the Pacific islands they had invaded, destroyed military installations on mainland Japan, and dropped atom bombs on Hiroshima and Nagasaki in 1945. The B-29 was a big plane, with a length of 99 feet and a wingspan of 141 feet. It could carry a bomb load of 10 tons and was a suitable design for conversion to the cargo role.

*The C-97, seen here as a tanker plane known as KC-97, saw wide use.*

*With an enlarged fuselage, the Boeing B-29 Superfortress was adapted into the C-97 cargo plane.*

Known as the C-97 Stratofreighter, the converted B-29 first flew in November 1944 and entered service with the U.S.A.F. *Military Air Transport Service (MATS)* in 1947. The plane had the same wingspan as the B-29, but fuselage length was increased to 117 feet. The fuselage was the most revolutionary part of the design. Instead of the tubular fuselage of the B-29, the C-97 had two tubular fuselages joined together. This gave the plane a figure-eight appearance but increased cargo volume.

The Stratofreighter could carry 96 fully equipped combat troops, 69 stretcher patients and their medical attendants, or 10 tons of cargo. It arrived in time to help out with the Berlin Airlift, and 888 of this type were built before production ended in

*The Douglas C-124 was an attempt to increase the lift capacity for long-range intercontinental duty.*

1956. The majority were converted to serve as aerial refueling tankers for *Strategic Air Command's* large force of long-range bombers.

The first transport plane wholly developed after World War Two was a stretched and improved version of the C-74, which had been canceled after only 14 entered service. The stretched version of the C-74 was called the C-124 Globemaster II and entered service at the beginning of the Korean War in 1950. This plane was built to lift tanks, guns, rockets, and missiles across long distances, and it provided for the air force a truly intercontinental cargo plane. With a length of 130 feet, a wingspan of 174 feet, and a height of 48 feet, it looked every bit the heavy lifter it was.

Globemaster II was a very big improvement on its predecessors. It could take most army equipment in its big fuselage, and it could lift a maximum 37 tons over short range. A typical load of 25 tons could be airlifted 2,300 miles at 230 MPH or 13 tons could be airlifted a distance of just over 4,000 miles. The Globemaster II could carry 200 fully equipped troops or 127 stretcher patients, as well as the medical staff and equipment to look after them.

The C-124 proved valuable in the Korean War (1950-53). Although the air force received only 396 planes of this type, it remained in service until 1970, when it was one of the oldest piston-engine designs to serve with the air force. The C-124 had one further development that eased loading. A large nose split in two halves to open and allow cargo to pass straight in to the open fuselage. Because of its likeness to a clam, its doors were called *clamshell doors*.

*Seen here on a C-5, the upward-hinging nose has made a major improvement to moving cargo quickly in and out of the aircraft.*

# Freighters

*The C-130 is designed to operate from rough, unpaved fields all over the world.*

The series of air force cargo planes operated since World War Two has evolved into a group of transport aircraft built for a broad range of duties. Between 1945 and 1950, cargo-lifting capacity went up from the 16 tons carried by the C-54 to the 37 tons transported by the C-124. All were powered by piston engines and belonged to the 1940s era of aircraft design. Beginning in the early 1950s, the air force and the army looked at gaps that appeared in the transport fleet.

They wanted a plane that could carry 92 combat troops, airdrop 64 fully equipped paratroopers, or move 74 stretcher cases. The plane would have to lift up to 12 tons of cargo and, if necessary, drop that load out the back on parachutes. It would require a range of more than 2,000 miles and a cruising speed

*For many years the medium-haul cargo lifter of the U.S. Air Force has been the Lockheed C-130 Hercules.*

*As an all-purpose transport plane, the C-130 has long range, reliability, and is easy to operate.*

of 350 MPH. In other words, it was to be a multi-role transport plane capable of delivering troops and cargo to the front line quickly and efficiently.

The aircraft built for this demanding job was the Lockheed C-130 Hercules, affectionately known as the *Herky-Bird*. In its day it was to become as much the workhorse of air transport as the Douglas DC-3 had been in the 1930s and 1940s. The Hercules had one big advantage over all previous transport planes. It was the first cargo plane operated by the air force designed from the beginning to use four *turboprop engines* made by the Allison company. More efficient than *piston engines*, these turboprops provided the secret ingredient for the C-130 to play a wide range of roles in its long service life.

The C-130 was designed so that its crew compartment and cargo hold could be pressurized throughout the flight. It had a strong wing attached to the top of the fuselage, giving good clearance below. To make cargo loading easier, the fuselage was set only 45 inches from the ground. The spacious cargo hold would take freight measuring 40 feet long by 10 feet by 9 feet. In all, the plane was 98 feet long with a span of 132 feet. Above all, the plane would be able to fly in and out of rough landing strips, greatly easing the problems of bringing cargo into remote areas.

*The C-130, also known as the Hercules, has been modified into an in-flight refueling tanker.*

The Hercules first flew in August 1954 and entered service just two years later. By the late 1980s, Lockheed had delivered around 1,000 to the air force alone. Using the military specifications for a tactical cargo lifter, Lockheed developed the C-130 into a general transport plane for export. They sold many to foreign air forces and made improvements to the design dictated by flying experience and added tasks. The C-130 played a major role in Vietnam, and the air force currently operates about 740 Herky-Birds.

Developed at about the same time as the C-130, the Douglas C-133 Cargomaster was an answer to deficiencies with existing cargo planes built to carry very heavy loads. Experience with the Berlin Airlift and the Korean War showed the need for a long-range, heavy-lift cargo plane capable of transporting bulky freight. The C-133 was built for easy access. It could gobble up cargo through a rear-loading door, and vehicles up to 12 feet tall and 11 feet, 10 inches wide could drive straight into the 90-foot-long bay.

When the Douglas Aircraft Company, later McDonnell Douglas, drew up designs for the C-133, the air force ordered a production version without even waiting for a prototype to be built and demonstrated. This was most unusual, because large, expensive planes must ordinarily prove their worth and value in the air before contracts are

*This Hercules is operating with the air force as a specially instrumented weather plane.*

*Operated by many air units, including the U.S. Coastguard, the C-130 has proved to be a versatile asset to air forces around the world.*

*One of the last major propeller-driven transport planes, the Douglas C-133 Cargomaster first appeared in the 1950s.*

placed for production. The C-133 first flew in 1956 and entered service three years later. At the time, it was the heaviest cargo plane in the air force.

Like the C-130, the Cargomaster had four turboprop engines, built for this plane by Pratt and Whitney. The C-133 was built in two versions, the second having the greatest lifting capacity. It could carry 26 tons over a distance of 4,000 miles and maintain a cruising speed of 323 MPH. With this plane, the air force could transport by air a complete Atlas intercontinental ballistic missile (*ICBM*), or Jupiter and Thor *intermediate-range missiles*. When they entered service, the C-133s were a great

improvement on the lifting capacity of the C-74s and C-124s they were intended to replace.

Along with the older types of transport planes, the Cargomaster was widely used in Vietnam. Oddly, it was outlived by the planes it was intended to replace. Widespread metal fatigue led to the C-133's early retirement from the air force, and by 1971 all 50 Cargomasters had been withdrawn. While some

C-124 Globemaster IIs were sold off to civilian cargo carriers, the C-133 was declared unserviceable due to fatigue. It was the end of a glorious career for Douglas transport planes. Not for 15 years would another Douglas plane operate with the air force as a cargo carrier.

Douglas had been the traditional builder of transport and cargo planes for more than 35 years. They had taken the military transport plane from the era of the twin-engined DC-3, lifting 6 tons, to the mighty Cargomaster, capable of carrying 26 tons across the world's great oceans. After World War Two, Lockheed entered the world of military transport with the C-69 and the C-121. These were military transport versions of the Constellation, a commercial airliner. The last C-121 was finally retired in 1968.

*The main purpose of the C-130 is to support troops in the field and assist ground operations by supplying equipment at short notice.*

*The Douglas C-118 was a converted DC-6 airliner; it never saw major operational duty.*

*The Lockheed C-69 was developed as an airliner and later used by the air force as troop-carrying transport plane.*

Following their success with the C-130 Hercules, Lockheed began working with the air force on a jet-powered heavy-transport plane during 1960. At that time the air force only had the piston-engined Boeing C-97, Douglas C-118 and C-124, and a few Lockheed C-121s. The C-118 was an old Douglas DC-6 airliner converted to carry about 13 tons of freight. The Douglas C-133 Cargomaster had just made its first flight, but it would be some time before it reached the air force. When it did, it would still not carry the loads the air force needed for fast, long-distance delivery.

The name of the transport wing of the U.S. Air Force had been changed from Military Air Transport Service to *Military Airlift Command (MAC)*. What MAC wanted was a jet cargo plane, and Lockheed provided that in the form of the C-141 Starlifter. It had a fuselage 145 feet long, a wingspan of 160 feet, and a distinctive T-shaped tail. Like the C-130, the C-141 had a high-mounted wing on top of the fuselage and four Pratt and Whitney *turbofan engines*, each producing 10.5 tons of thrust.

The first version, the C-141A, had a cargo bay 70 feet long, 10 feet wide, and 9 feet high. For cargo loading, a clamshell door was provided at the rear with a ramp along which vehicles could travel to the interior of the cargo hold. The Starlifter could carry 138 troops in rear-facing seats, 80 stretcher cases and attendants, or 32 tons of cargo. Maximum range with a full load was just over 4,000 miles, but with a cruising speed of 480 MPH it could arrive several hours ahead of the Douglas C-133.

*Built by Lockheed, the C-141 Starlifter was the first long-range jet transport plane.*

Starlifter started rolling off the production line in December 1963. Two years later it was operational with MAC, and by 1968 all 285 planes had been delivered. Some had strengthened *airframes* that allowed the fuselage to carry extra weight. The air force wanted to lift fully-assembled *Minuteman* ICBMs around the country. To do that, the Starlifter's carrying capacity was increased to 43 tons.

Starlifter had hardly entered service with MAC when it was called upon to play an important role. It had to begin the movement of masses of men, cargo, and machines to southeast Asia. The war in Vietnam was heating up, and other cargo planes could not do the job. Most westbound flights to Vietnam departed from Travis Air Force Base in California. On their return from each delivery mission, they brought injured men and others on leave from the grim job of war. During 1968, Starlifters flew more than 10,000 troops and 5,100 tons of equipment from Fort Campbell, Kentucky, to Bien Hoa, Vietnam, when a major communist offensive threatened to overthrow U.S. bases.

*The Starlifter has carried out heavy duty in rugged country in all kinds of weather.*

*The C-141 has rear opening doors allowing cargo to be moved straight in and out along the fuselage when the plane is on the ground.*

Bringing back casualties was to account for 6,000 of the C-141's aeromedical missions between 1965 and 1972. That represents more than 16 flights each week for 7 years. The C-141 was also called upon to fly home the 588 prisoners of war released by the communist Vietnamese in 1973 and to fly out the refugees in 1975. In contrast, a C-141 was used to carry a special isolation van to greet the astronauts after the first Apollo moon landing in 1969. The van kept them isolated in quarantine for several weeks to be sure they had not brought any diseases back to earth.

Starlifters also flew 421 missions and delivered 10,000 tons of combat equipment and supplies to the Israeli armed forces when the Arabs attacked in 1973 during a Middle East war. In 1978, C-141 planes airlifted 5,800 passengers and 687 tons of cargo from Iran when the Shah was overthrown by the revolution that brought Ayatollah Khomeini to power. In October 1983, Starlifter evacuated 709 American and foreign nationals from the Caribbean when U.S. troops landed to restore order on the island of Grenada.

The lessons of Vietnam pointed to two

*The Starlifter has long range and has carried out many duties in Southeast Asia.*

*The range of the C-141 is further extended by the use of in-flight refueling tankers.*

capabilities still missing from Military Airlift Command. The air force needed a transport with an even larger carrying capacity, and the capability for in-flight refueling was an essential part of flying long-range missions. There was no money to develop a completely new plane, so Lockheed was asked by the air force to modify the C-141A series planes into a new variant, the C-141B. This model would be 23 feet longer than the previous version and would be able to lift almost 45 tons a distance of 3,200 miles. With an *in-flight refueling probe* added as standard, it could be filled by a tanker and fly half way around the world.

The C-141B was 168 feet long and could accommodate up to 208 troops or 168 paratroops.

Lockheed began modifying 270 existing Starlifters into the "B" version in 1978, and by 1982 the last had been sent back for duty with MAC. The increased lifting capacity and performance was equivalent to 90 extra aircraft the air force did not have to buy. One aircraft was delivered to *NASA*, the space agency, for special use at high altitude as an airborne laboratory. Today, about 250 Starlifters are in service with the air force. The C-141B remains the principal heavy-lift cargo plane, along with the Lockheed C-5 Galaxy, the biggest U.S. transport plane of them all.

*Large numbers of Starlifters helped move troops back and forth between the United States and Vietnam during the war of the 1960s and the early 1970s.*

# The Giants

The original specification that resulted in development of the C-141 Starlifter had been started by President John F. Kennedy. In exchange for reductions in the number of men and materials overseas, the President increased the readiness of units at home to go abroad if the need arose. The C-141 specification was set down in part to fulfill that need for greater transport capacity to move troops in time of crisis. Unfortunately, the

*The Galaxy has an upward-hinging nose to allow the easy passage of heavy cargo through the front.*

specification failed to provide sufficient space in the plane for the biggest pieces of army equipment.

To build the right kind of plane for carrying the heaviest pieces of military equipment, like tanks and howitzers, the air force began a program in 1963 to

*The biggest transport plane operated by the U.S. Air Force is the Lockheed C-5 Galaxy.*

decide on the right specification. It chose a design from Lockheed for what came to be called the C-5 Galaxy program. It was to result in a gigantic airplane with a maximum takeoff weight of 384.5 tons, more than twice the takeoff weight of the Starlifter.

*Several small fighter planes can be carried inside the huge cargo hold of the C-5.*

*A special ramp folds up inside the cargo hold.*

When it was flown for the first time in June 1968, the Galaxy was surprisingly like the C-141 Starlifter. It was, of course, much bigger. It was 247 feet, 10 inches long, had a wing span of 222 feet, 8 inches, and stood more than 65 feet tall to the tip of its enormous tail. Cargo and freight would be carried in a very large bay that took up the entire length of the fuselage inside. The bay had a length of 121 feet, a height of 13 feet, 6 inches, and a width of 19 feet.

The Galaxy could carry anything the army wanted to move. It had clamshell doors at the rear and, for the first time on a production aircraft, an upward-hinging nose. Freight could be loaded off at the back and on at the front in one continuous operation. It had space in an upper deck for a relief crew of 15 in addition to the five carried on the flight deck. It could also carry 75 troops in the upper deck and 290 in the main cargo bay for a total 365.

The cavernous cargo bay was more than five times the size of the Starlifter's bay. The enormous wing had a surface area of 6,000 square feet, and overall the plane was bigger than a Jumbo Jet. It stood on 28 wheels — 4 on the nose landing leg and 6 on each of 4 main landing legs fitted to the center fuselage. This strange undercarriage arrangement was designed to meet one of the plane's demanding specifications. In addition to carrying enormous loads great distances, the Galaxy had to operate from semi-prepared airfields. This implied it would have to land and take off from rough strips and that made it necessary to spread its enormous weight so as not to bog down.

*When lowered to the ground, the forward ramp allows easy access into the plane.*

*Despite its size, the C-5 is a good plane to fly and handles well.*

*Large pallets of cargo can be moved into the Galaxy through the rear.*

Power was provided by four huge turbofan engines built by General Electric, each of which delivered more than 20 tons of thrust. Enormous fuel tanks, fed to these economical engines, helped keep the Galaxy in the air for up to 17 hours at an average cruising speed of 518 MPH. Without cargo it could fly 8,400 miles non-stop on internal fuel. Empty, the Galaxy C-5A weighed over 150 tons, more than the fully loaded weight of a Starlifter.

Maximum cargo load for the C-5A was a phenomenal 133 tons, bringing maximum takeoff weight with fuel on board to a staggering 384 tons. With maximum load in the cargo bay, range was 3,750 miles, or 6,530 miles with 56 tons on board. In December 1984, a Galaxy set a U.S. record for the heaviest cargo load by an airplane when it took off with 123 tons on board. At takeoff, the plane weighed 460 tons, also a record.

The first operational Galaxy was delivered to Military Airlift Command in December 1969. Since then 81 C-5As have been built for the air force. The Galaxy arrived too late to have a real effect on logistics in the Vietnam War, but it has played an important part since in the mass movement of men and supplies all over the world. It is particularly useful on the Pacific routes where, for only a little less lifting capacity, it can readily span the ocean with ease.

One major drawback with the Galaxy was the

early onset of structural fatigue in the wings, not an uncommon occurrence with heavy transport planes. Fatigue on the C-5s was particularly bad, however, and Lockheed was awarded a contract in 1978 to completely re-design the wings. Eventually, all Galaxies got new wings to give them a new lease on life. The last Galaxy to get its wings was returned to duty in 1987.

Despite the C-5A's tremendous lifting capacity,

*To support its weight on the ground, the Galaxy has a large number of wheels that help spread the weight.*

*The largest cargo plane of all is this Soviet Antonov An-124.*

*The C-5 is being built in increasing numbers to help move U.S. armed forces anywhere in the world.*

the air force wanted even more for its overseas duties. The C-5B, a modified Galaxy, was ordered. Lockheed delivered the first in 1986 and completed the production run three years later. The C-5B has more powerful engines than the C-5A and has incorporated many improvements and modifications that had been applied to earlier C-5A models

in past years. With added lifting capacity demanded by heavier equipment, the C-5B can carry more than 145 tons, and maximum takeoff weight is now 418 tons.

The new Galaxy can carry 2 Abrams tanks, 6 Apache attack helicopters, 10 Pershing missiles, or 64 cargo pallets. With this enormous carrying capacity, Galaxy is set to remain the mainstay of MAC well into the next century. Yet it is no longer the biggest aircraft in the world — Russia's Antonov An-124 Condor is only slightly bigger in size but can

37

*The Soviets operate a wide range of cargo planes to support their military needs.*

lift 165 tons. It has a maximum range of more than 10,000 miles on internal fuel.

If the C-5 Galaxy is the heavy-lift transport plane for carrying men and material primarily for the army, the McDonnell Douglas KC-10 Extender is the one the air force uses to ferry its combat planes to far-off places. This role fell to other planes in the past, but in the late 1970s, it became more important.

At that time, President Jimmy Carter ordered the air force to look at the possibility of moving military forces overseas much more quickly than before. This was to fit in with his concept of "rapid deployment," the rapid movement of forces from the U.S. to foreign countries when aggression threatened to upset the peace. In a way, it was similar to the policy laid down by Kennedy almost 20 years before.

The air force had operated tanker planes since the 1950s, when in-flight refueling of heavy bombers was a very good way to extend their range. The need

arose when events like the Berlin Airlift indicated a continuing need for long-range access to foreign countries. Taking the basic transport planes of the day, the air force made them into *tanker planes.* Instead of cargo and freight, they carried extra fuel tanks in the fuselage.

When converted for tanker duty, the normal "C" designation was prefixed with a "K" so that when some C-97 Stratofreighters were converted to tankers they were designated KC-97. Similarly, when the C-135 transporter was made into a tanker it became the KC-135. The C-135 was a transport version of the Boeing 707, the world's first successful jet airliner. The Strategic Air Command was responsible for all the bombers in the air force and

*One of the latest cargo planes in operational service is the McDonnell Douglas KC-10.*

*The KC-10 doubles as a tanker plane in addition to carrying large amounts of cargo.*

*The KC-10 is a developed version of the DC-10 airliner in wide use around the world.*

operated approximately 600 KC-135 tankers for almost 20 years; in the 1980s the numbers dropped to around 500.

Combining the need to replace the old KC-135s and give new muscle to air fighter units in *Tactical Air Command*, the air force went after a new tanker that would have much greater capability than earlier tankers. In 1977 they chose a modified version of the McDonnell Douglas DC-10 commercial airliner and gave it the name KC-10A Extender. It would be capable of lifting 50 tons of freight almost 7,000 miles or 85 tons a distance of almost 4,400 miles. Alternatively, it could serve as a tanker plane. Without cargo on board, the Extender could ferry itself a distance of 11,500 miles on internal fuel.

The real value of the Extender is its ability to fly several fighter planes across the Atlantic Ocean in one mission — not by carrying them inside the cargo bay but by periodically refilling their tanks in mid-air via three in-flight refueling probes. The cargo-carrying capacity is split between fuel for the jet fighters and stores, mechanics, and supplies necessary to maintain the planes and keep them

41

operating when they reach their destination. This is a completely new capability for the air force, made possible only by the size of the KC-10A Extender.

The KC-10A can be fitted out as cargo plane, tanker, or both together. Up to 18,125 gallons of fuel, weighing approximately 58.9 tons, is carried in seven rubberized fuel tanks in the cargo hold. Made by Goodyear, these tanks supply fuel to three probes. One is in the tail of the plane and one under each wing. A special refueling station in the tail gives operating crew members a good view of the refueling planes as they come up to be filled.

The Extender has a length of 182 feet, a wing span of 165 feet, 4 inches, and a tail tip height of 58 feet. It is powered by three General Electric turbofan engines, each producing 26 tons of thrust at takeoff. Extender has a maximum fueled weight of 295 tons and a cruising speed of 575 MPH. The plane is more than 55 MPH faster than the Galaxy, and for some missons it has a better range with equivalent payload. The Galaxy is a worthy marriage of the cargo role with the tanker role that has, until now, required a separate conversion.

The first Extender for the air force was delivered to Seymour Johnson Air Force Base near Goldsboro, North Carolina, in October 1985. Initial orders totaled 60 planes by the end of the 1980s, although additional orders are expected in the 1990s. This plane is what the air force calls a *force multiplier*. In other words, its capacity to carry cargo, fuel, or a combination of both is so much greater than the planes it replaces that one aircraft is equal to several of the older type. The plane is more efficient and cost-effective.

*For really long-range jobs, a KC-10 refuels a C-5 Galaxy.*

# Future Freighters

*The McDonnell Douglas C-17 has been chosen as the next generation transport plane.*

The Lockheed C-130 Hercules is expected to have a long life ahead of it, and the Lockheed C-5A and B heavy transport planes are expected to remain on duty well into the next century. With these planes, Lockheed has made a significant contribution to air force cargo fleets. McDonnell Douglas has been chosen, however, to build the air force's next transport plane, to be called the C-17A. McDonnell Douglas is building a prototype and two test planes, and the air force expects to buy 210 planes of this type by 1999.

The C-17A will be capable of lifting outsize cargo like that currently carried aboard the C-5 Galaxy, yet it will have the rough field handling and performance of the C-130 Hercules. It will carry 86 tons of cargo a distance of 2,765 miles and land in only 3,000 feet of rough grassland. Or it can fly 65 tons a distance of 3,225 miles. The C-17A's combination of great lifting capacity and the ability to operate out of difficult airfields make it such a useful design.

The C-17 will be powered by four Pratt and Whitney turbofan engines, each delivering a thrust of 18.5 tons. The engines are carried in separate pods

under the high-mounted wing, giving the aircraft good handling characteristics in the air and ease of handling on the ground. The main undercarriage is housed in bulbous fairings on either side of the fuselage, leaving the interior free for cargo space.

It will operate out of rough grass runways only 3,000 feet long and 60 feet wide, and it will be able to make a complete turn in only 82 feet, allowing it to land, turn at the end of the runway and take off again along the way it came. It will be able to back up

*The C-17 is designed to carry troops as well as cargo.*

inclines and slopes to load and unload cargo, and it will be reliable, needing very little maintenance. As the next step beyond the C-130 Hercules, the C-17 will combine many features and performance capabilities usually found in separate transport planes.

44

The air force has come a long way since the Douglas transport planes staggered into the air with a few tons of cargo. Now McDonnell Douglas is once again working on a "first" with the C-17 design, which will prepare the armed services to carry out their work in the next century. No matter what the role of the air force becomes in the future, it will always need planes to shift cargo, move freight, and refuel planes in the sky.

*The new transport plane will operate in and out of unpaved fields far from conventional air bases.*

*The C-17 will supply troops and ground forces in remote parts of the world.*

# GLOSSARY

| | |
|---|---|
| Airframe | The structure of an aircraft, usually including the fuselage, wings, tail and internal support structures. |
| Berlin Airlift | The 1948-1949 relief operation in which transport planes from the United States and Britain air-lifted more than 2.2 million tons of supplies into Berlin when it was blockaded by the Soviets. |
| Clamshell doors | Doors that form the bulbous nose of a transport plane and split open, like a clamshell, for loading and unloading. |
| Force multiplier | An aircraft designed to replace and do the job of two or more older aircraft. |
| Herky-Bird | The popular name given to the Lockheed C-130 medium transport plane. |
| In-flight refueling probe | A fixed probe, usually attached to the nose of an aircraft, that can be connected with a flexible hose from a tanker plane to transfer fuel in flight. |
| Intercontinental Ballistic Missile (ICBM) | A missile designed to carry a nuclear warhead across intercontinental distances. |
| Intermediate range missiles | Missiles with less striking range than intercontinental missiles but greater than the range of smaller missiles used on battlefields. |
| Military Air Transport Service (MATS) | The former name for the cargo-carrying service operated by the United States Air Force; the name was changed to Military Airlift Command. |
| Military Airlift Command (MAC) | The present name of the U.S. Air Force command responsible for freight and cargo planes. |
| Minuteman | The long-range U.S. Air Force intercontinental ballistic missile fired from vertical underground silos. |
| National Aeronautics and Space Administration (NASA) | The United States government agency responsible for all major non-military space and aeronautical research projects. |
| Piston engine | An aircraft engine based on the principle of a reciprocating engine, like those used for automobiles, that drives a propeller or airscrew. |
| Strategic Air Command | The United States Air Force command responsible for the large fleet of long-range bombers, tanker planes, and ground launched missiles of intercontinental range. |
| Tactical Air Command | The U.S. Air Force organization responsible for the defense of the United States and for conducting limited conventional or nuclear war. |
| Tanker planes | Aircraft designed to carry special equipment for refueling other aircraft in flight. |
| Turbofan engine | Essentially a jet engine with a series of blades arranged in a circle like a fan to increase the amount of air being delivered to the combustion chamber where the fuel is fed in for burning. |

Turboprop engine    A jet engine with blades arranged in a circle like a fan to increase the amount of air delivered to the combustion chamber.

Wright brothers    Wilbur and Orville Wright, the two brothers who are credited with having developed and flown the first powered heavier-than-air machine in 1903.

# INDEX

Page references in *italics* indicate photographs or illustrations.

Antonov An-124 Condor — *36,* 37
Apache attack helicopter — 22
Atlas intercontinental ballistic
    missile (ICBM) — 22

Berlin Airlift — 11, 12, 15, 20, 38
Boeing: B-29 Superfortress — *13,* 15
    C-97 Stratofreighter — 15, 25, 38
    707 — 38

Carter, President Jimmy — 38
C-5 Galaxy — *6, 16,* 29, *31 32,*
    *33, ,34, 35, 36, 37,*
    38, *42,* 43
C-5A — 35, 36, 37, 43
C-5B — 37, 43
C-17 — *43, 44, 45*
C-17A — 43
C-47 — *7, 8, 9,* 11
C-54 Skymaster — 9, *10, 11,* 12, 17
C-69 — 23, *24*
C-74 Globemaster I — *12, 13,* 16, 22
C-97 Stratofreighter — *14,* 15, 25, 38
C-118 — *24,* 25
C-121 — 23, 25
C-124 Globemaster II — *15,* 16, 17, 22, 23,
    25
C-130 Hercules — *17, 18, 19, 20, 21,*
    22, 23, 25, 43, 44
C-133 Cargomaster — 20, 21, *22,* 23, 25
C-135 — 38
C-141 Starlifter — *25, 26, 27, 28, 29,*
    *30,* 32, 33
C-141A — 25, 29
C-141B — 29
Condor — *36,* 37
Constellation — 23

DC-3 Dakota — 9, 11, 23
DC-4 — *10,* 11
DC-10 — 41
Douglas: C-54 Skymaster — 9, *10, 11,* 12, 17
    C-74 Globemaster I — *12, 13,* 16, 22
    C-118 — *24,* 25
    C-124 — *15,* 16, 17, 22, 23,
    25
    C-133 Cargomaster — 20, 21, *22,* 23, 25
    DC-3 Dakota — 11, 19, 23
    DC-6 — 25

Galaxy — *6, 16,* 29, *31, 32,*
    *33, 34, 35, 36, 37,*
    38, *42,* 43

Hercules (Herky-Bird) — *17, 18, 19, 20, 21,*
    22, *23,* 25, 43, 44

KC-10 Extender — 38, *39, 40, 41, 42*
KC-10A Extender — 41, 42
KC-97 — *14,* 38
KC-135 — 38, 41
Kennedy, President John F. — 30, 38
Korean War — 16, 20

Lockheed: C-5 Galaxy — *6, 16,* 29, *31, 32,*
    *33, 34, 35, 36, 37,*
    38, *42,* 43
    C-5A Galaxy — 35, 36, 37, 43
    C-5B Galaxy — 37, 43
    C-69 — 23, *24*
    C-121 — 23, 25
    C-130 Hercules — *17, 18, 19, 20, 21,*
    22, 23, 25, 43, 44
    C-141 Starlifter — *25, 26, 27, 28, 29,*
    *30,* 32, 33
C-141A Starlifter — 25, 29
C-141B Starlifter — 29

McDonnell Douglas: C-17 — *43, 44, 45*
    C-17A — 43
    DC-10 — 41
    KC-10 Extender — 38, *39, 40, 41, 42*
    KC-10A Extender — 41, 42
Military Air Transport Service
    (MATS) — 15, 25
Military Airlift Command (MAC) — 25, 26, 29, 35, 37
Minuteman intercontinental
    ballistic missile (ICBM) — 26

NASA — 29

Pershing missile — 37
Pratt and Whitney — 22, 25, 43

Seymour Johnson Air Force Base — 42
Skymaster — 9, *10, 11,* 12, 17
Starlifter — *25, 26, 27, 28, 29,*
    *30,* 32, 33
Stratofreighter — *14,* 15, 25, 38
Superfortress — *13,* 15

Thor intermediate-range missile — 22
Travis Air Force Base — 26

Vietnam — 20, 22, 26, 27
Vietnam War — 35

World War Two — 7, 12, 16, 17, 23